Cute Princess Coloring Book, Beautiful Princesses

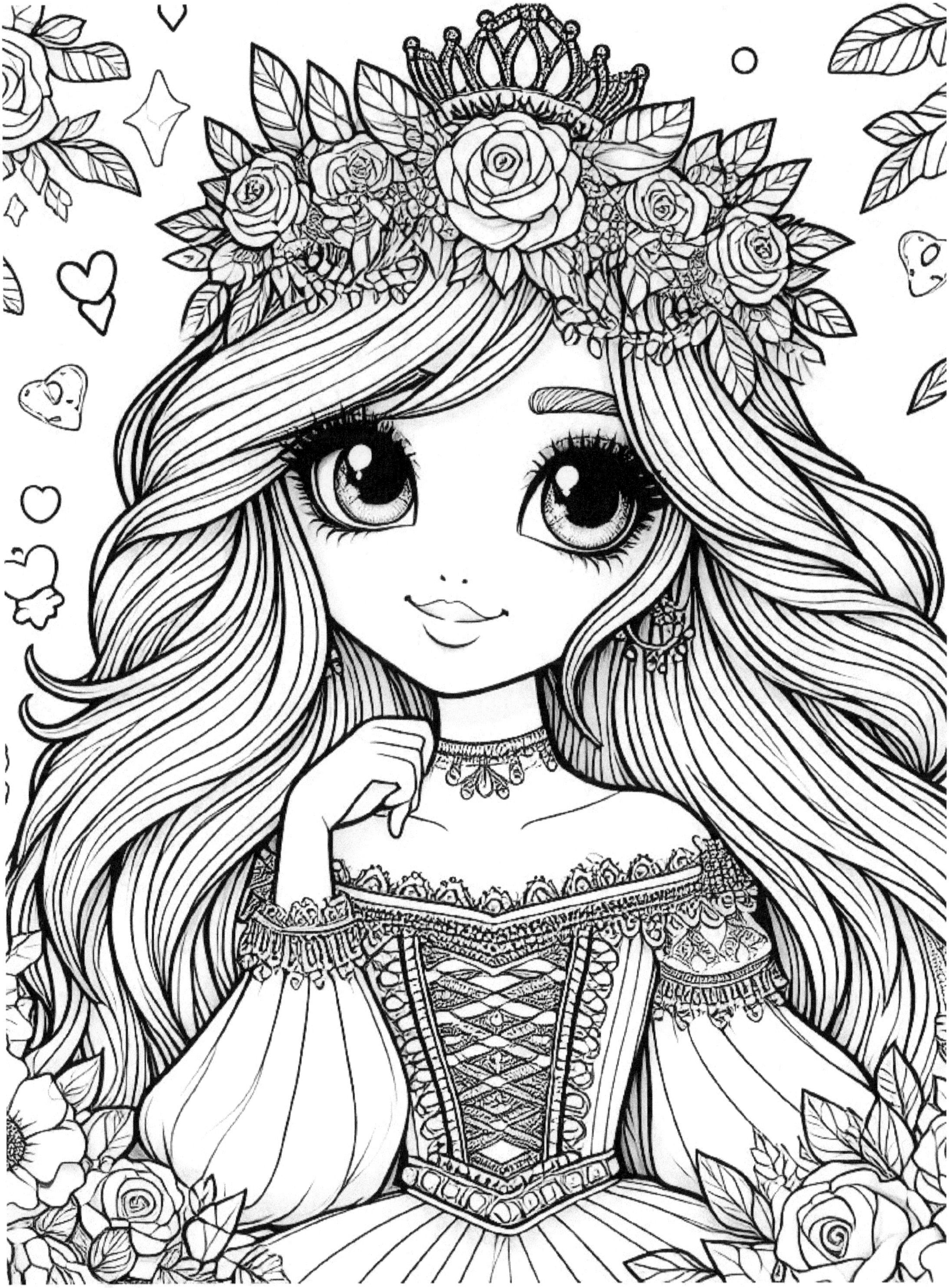

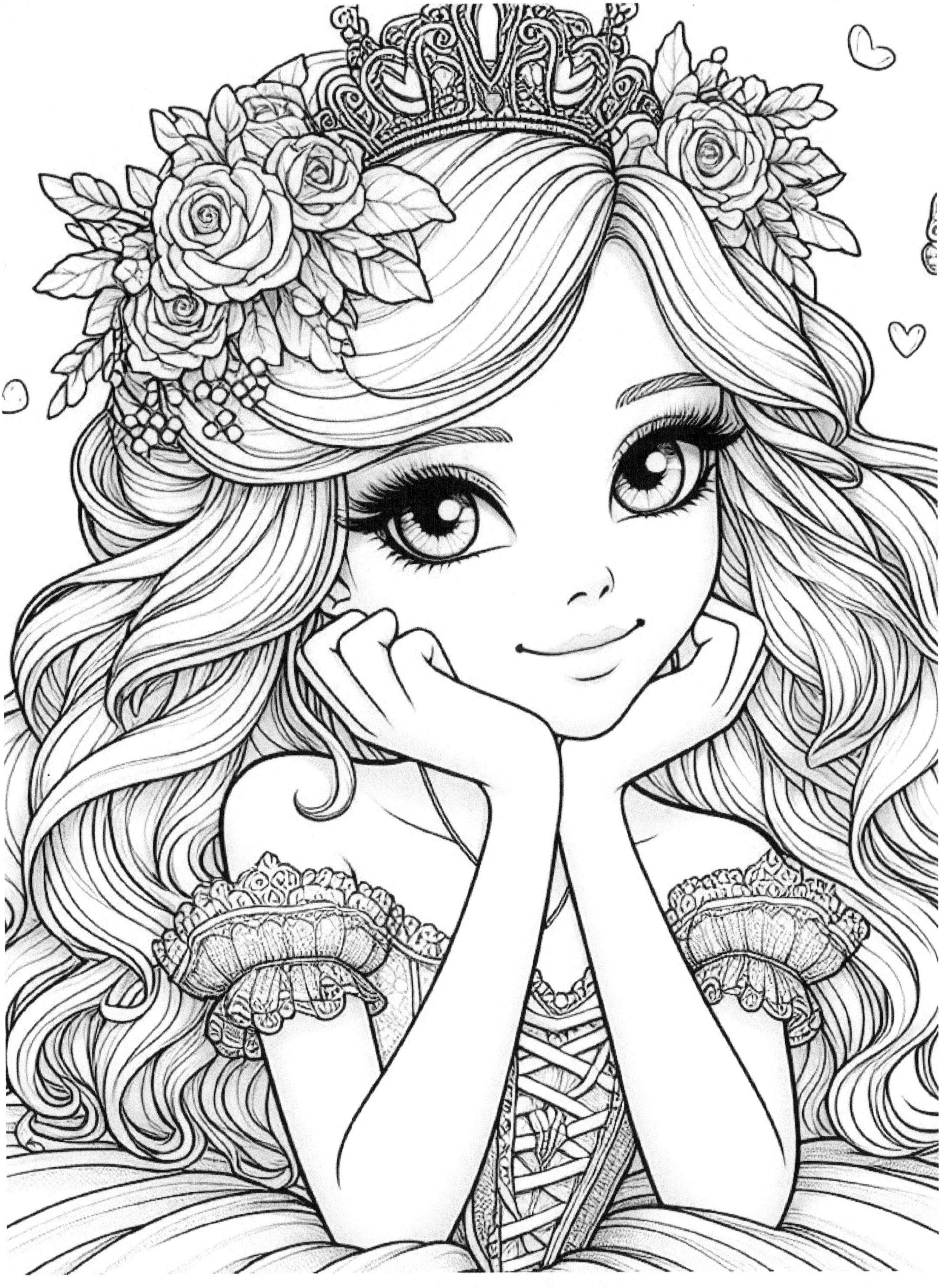

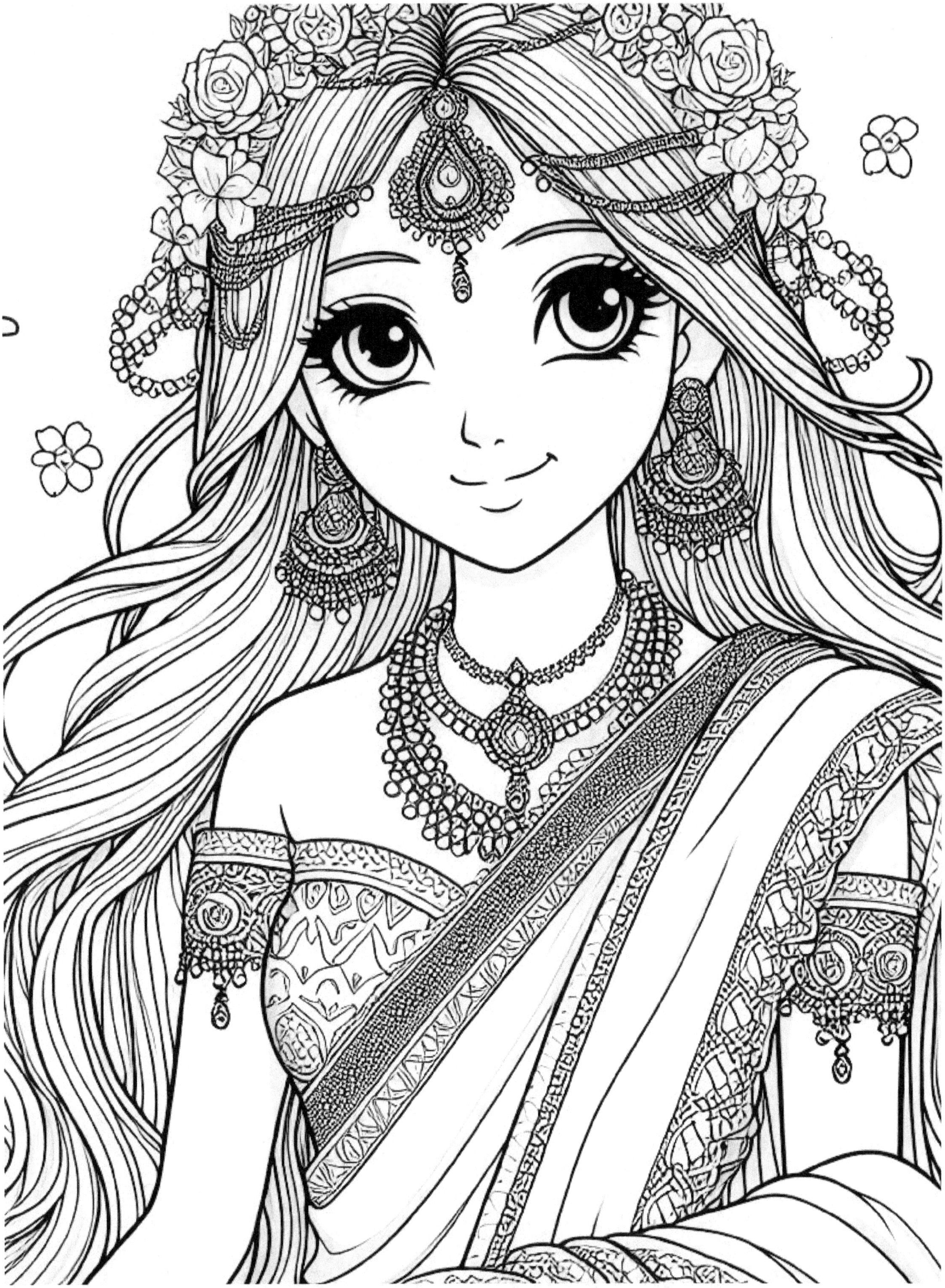

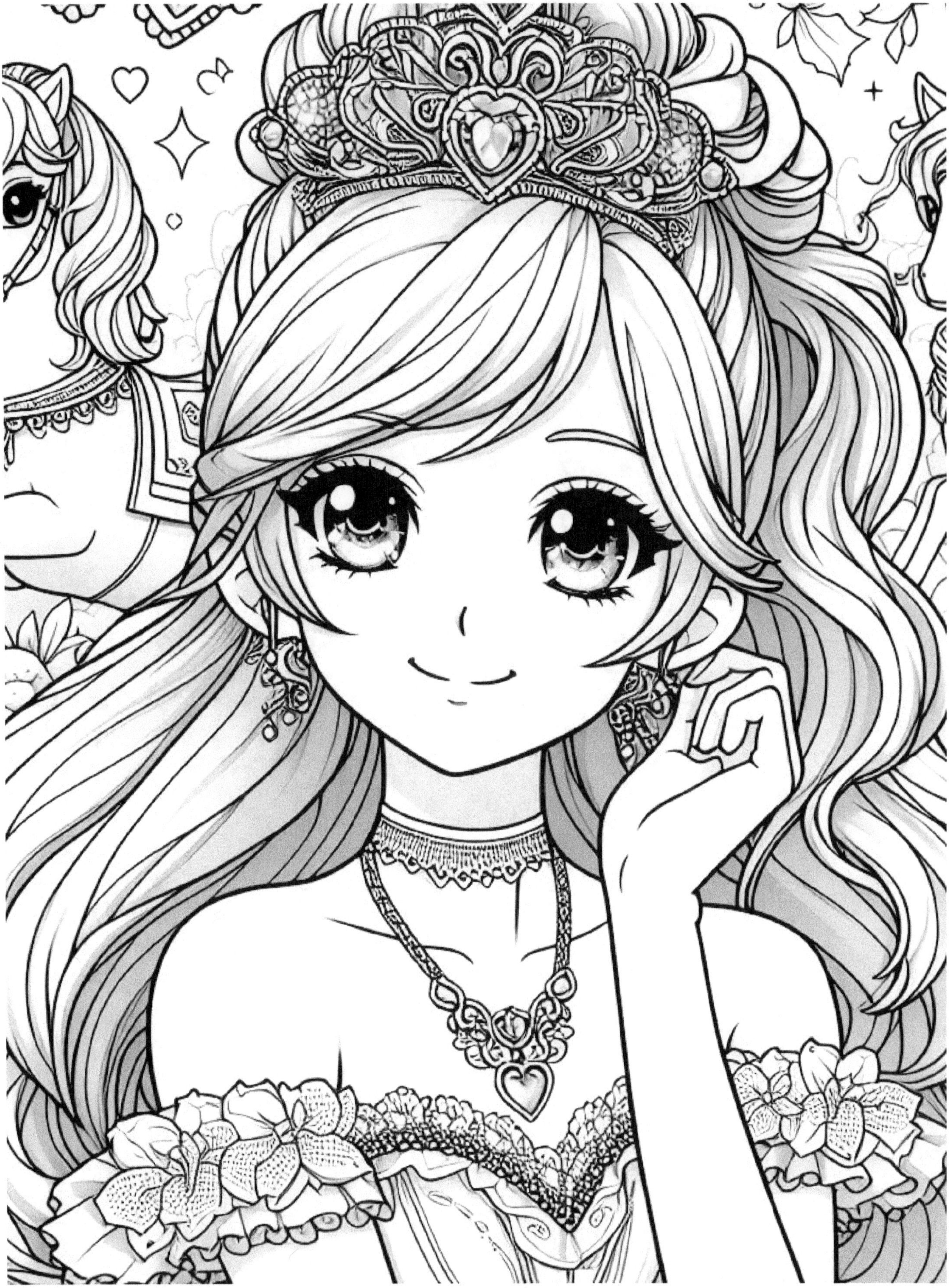

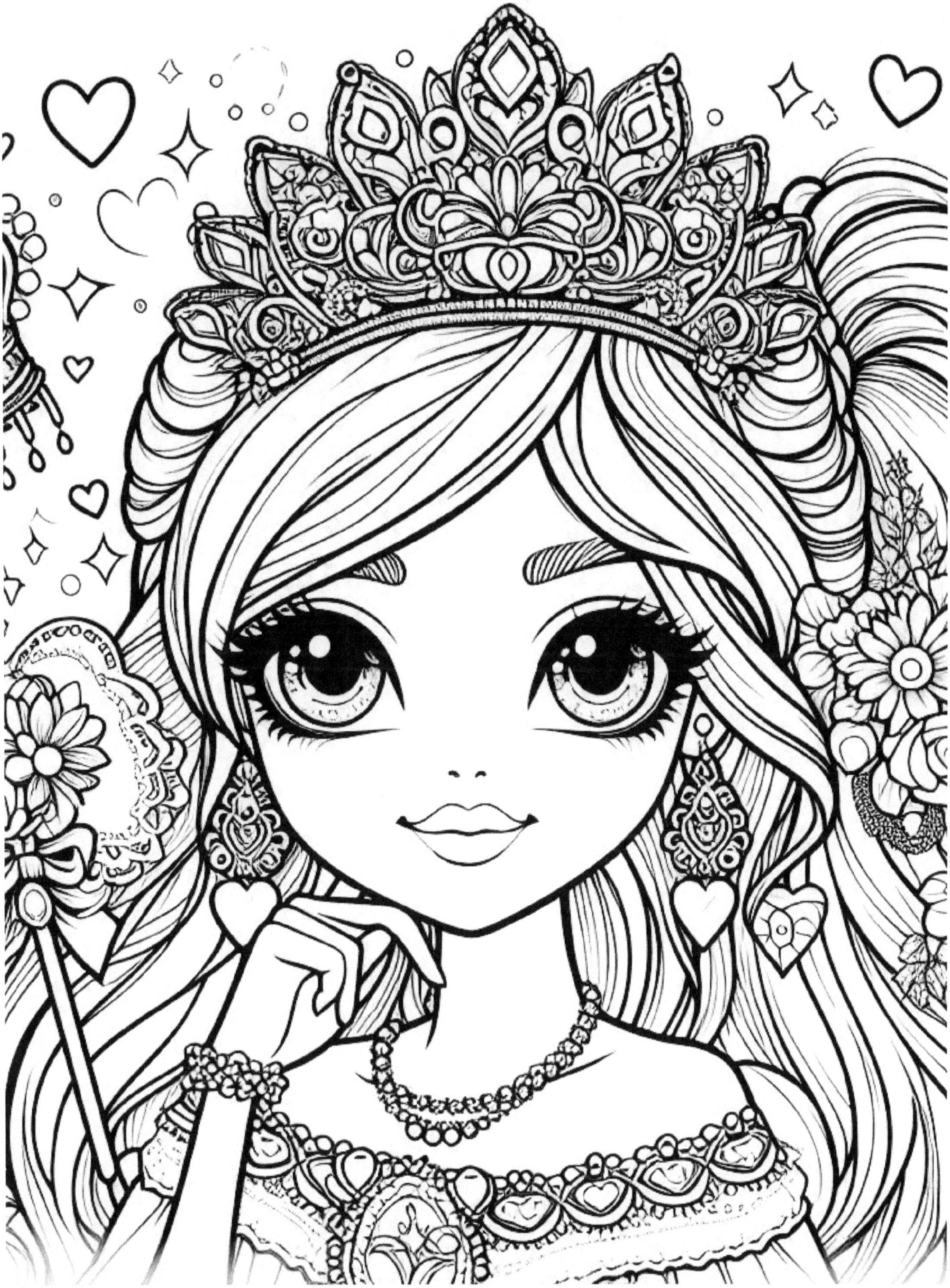

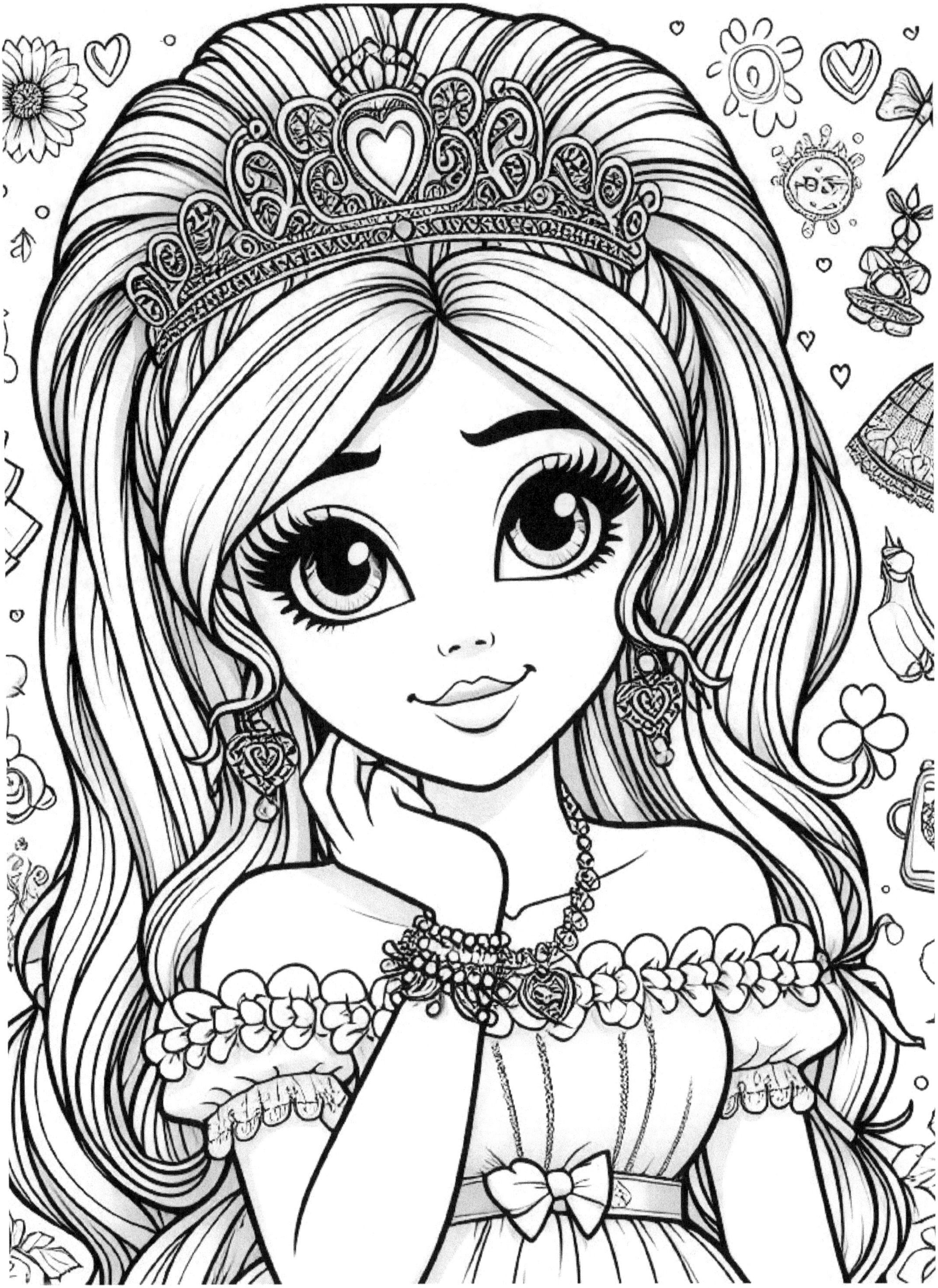

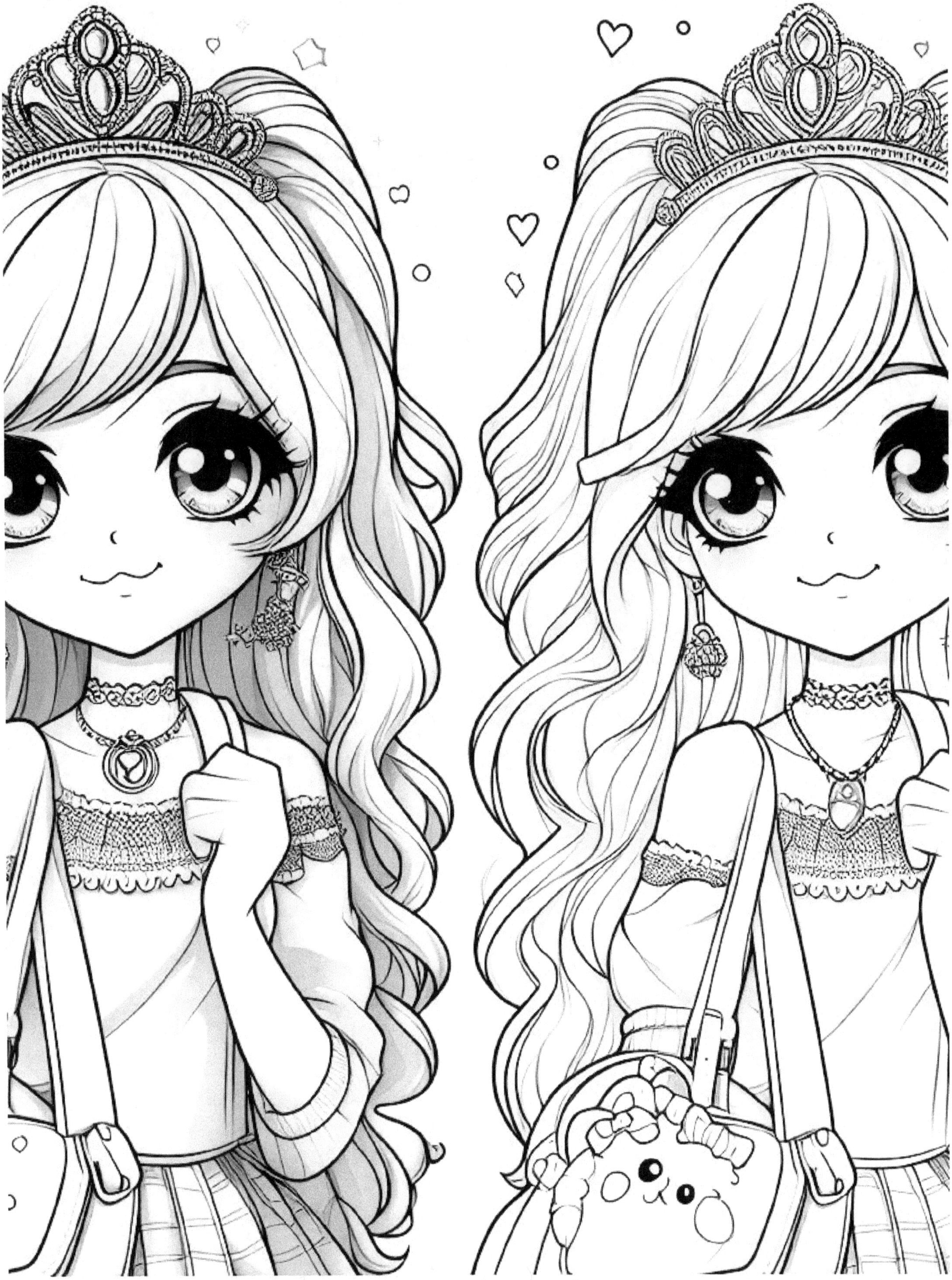

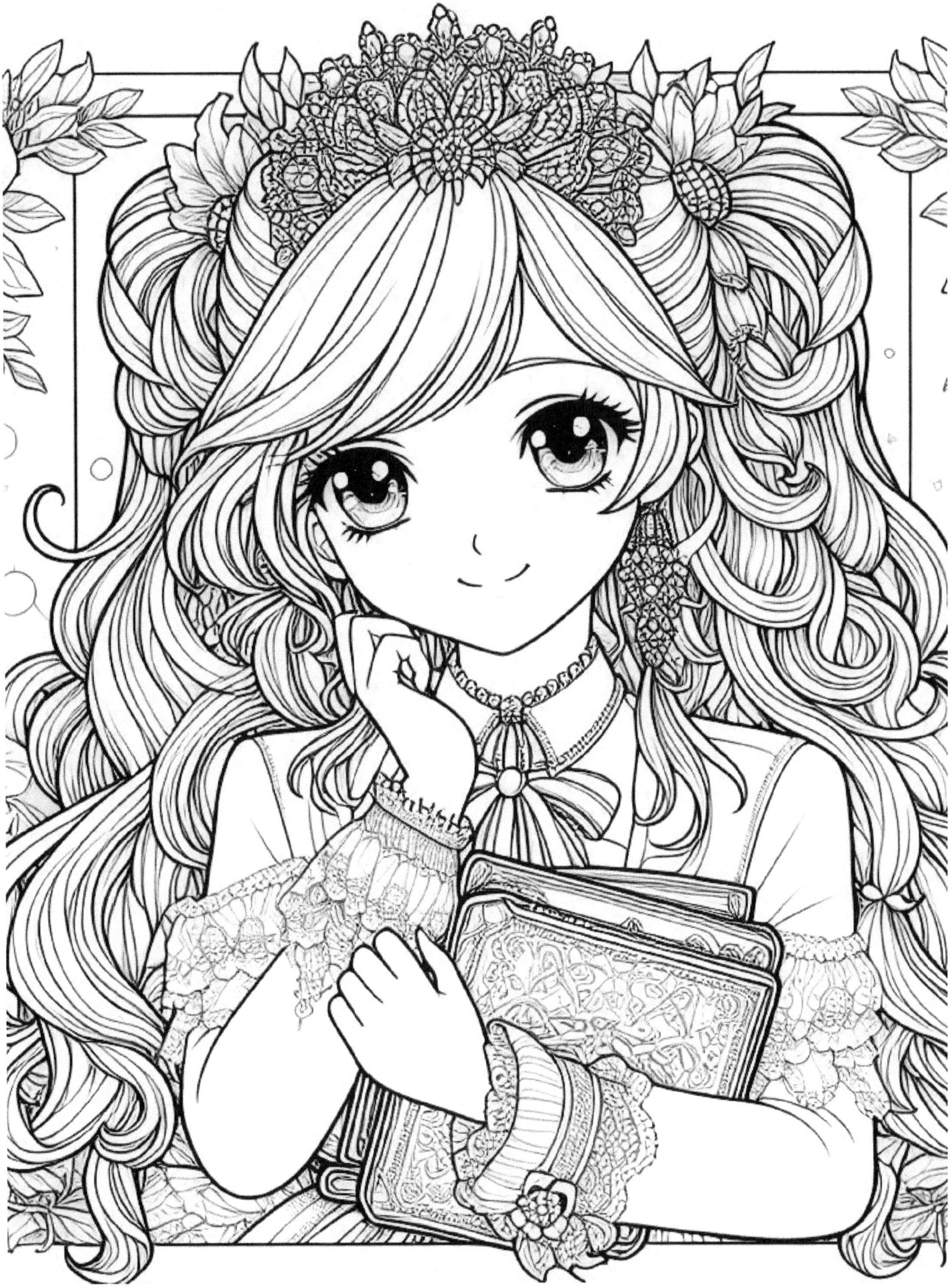

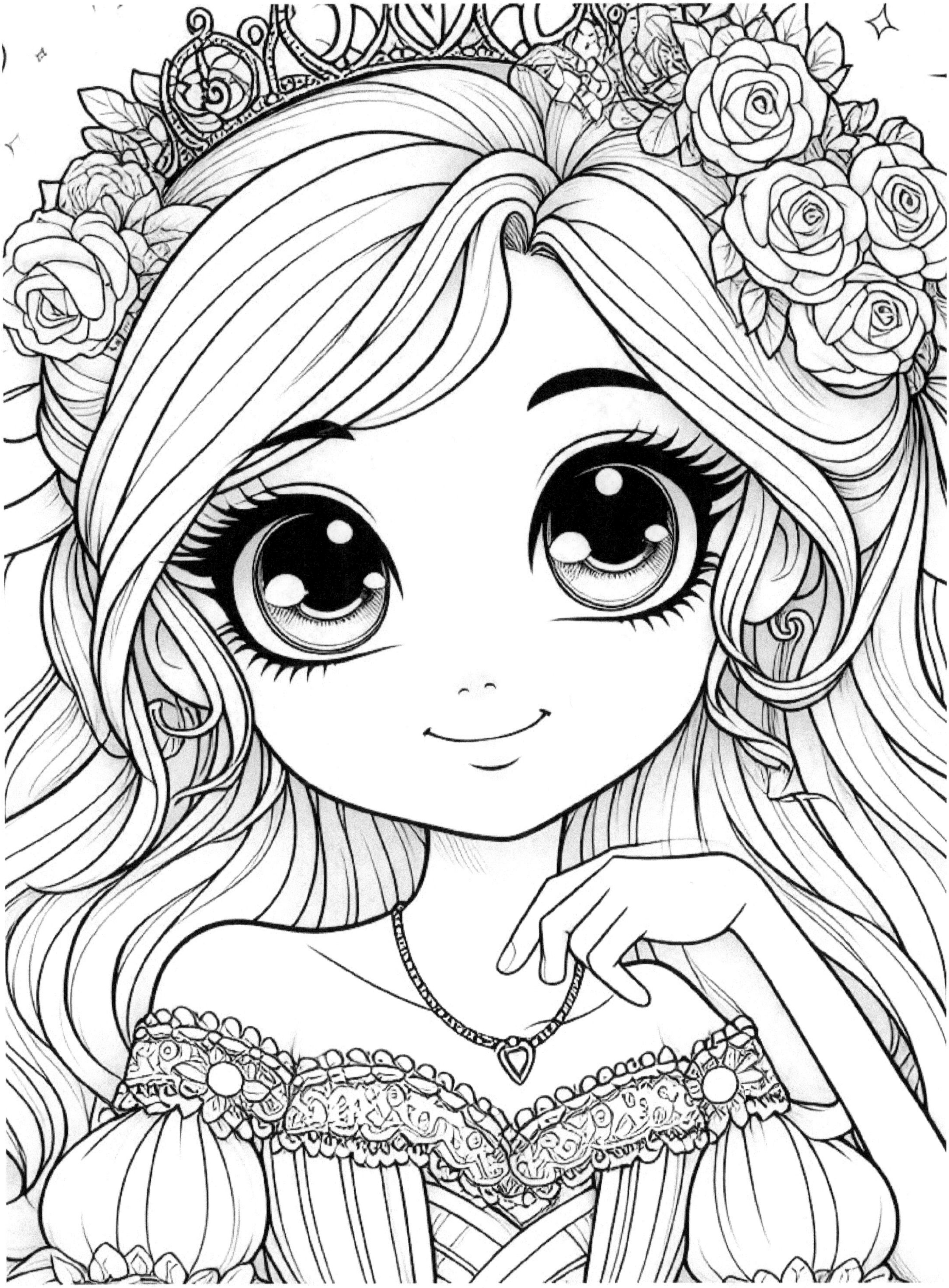

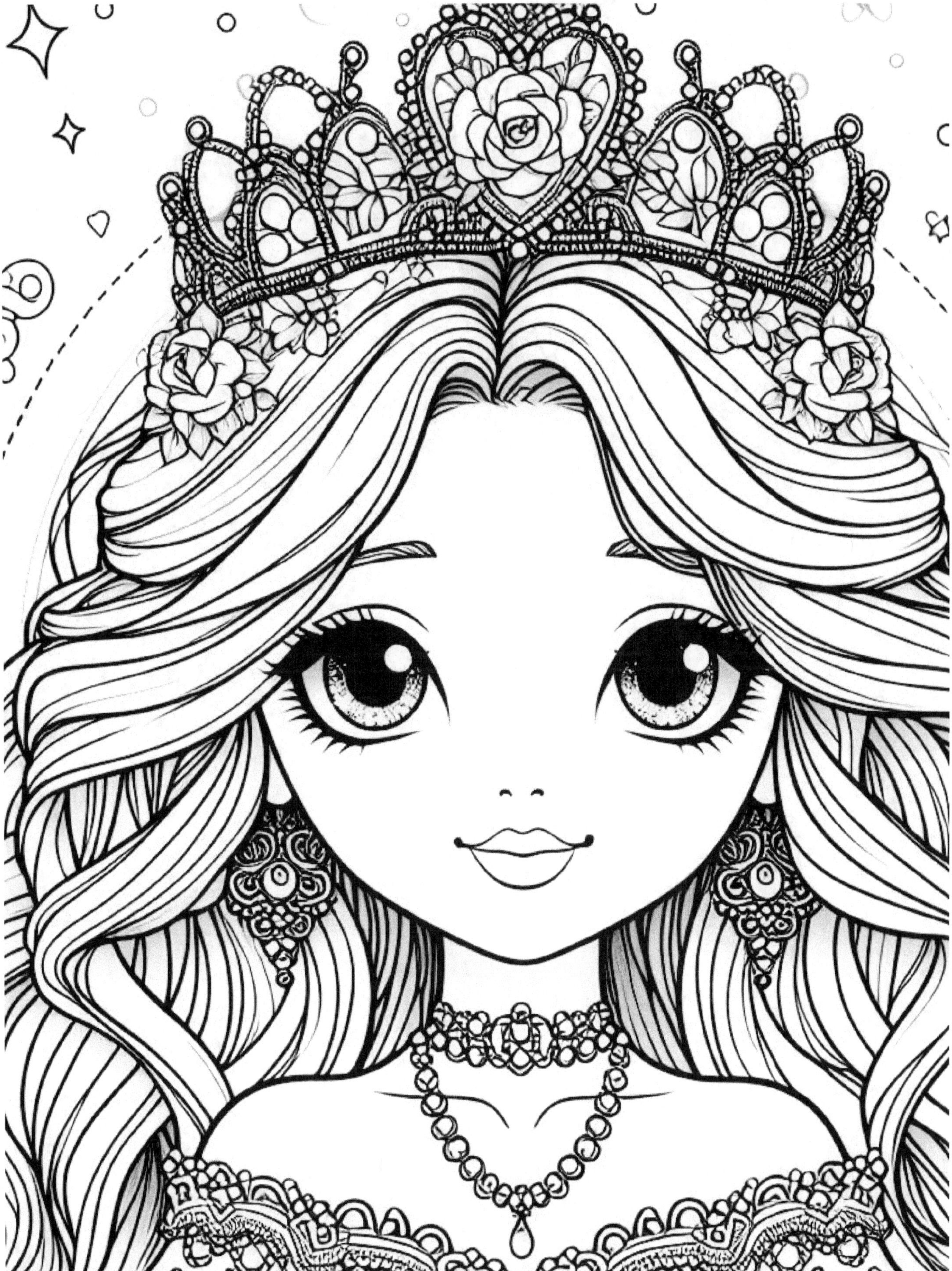

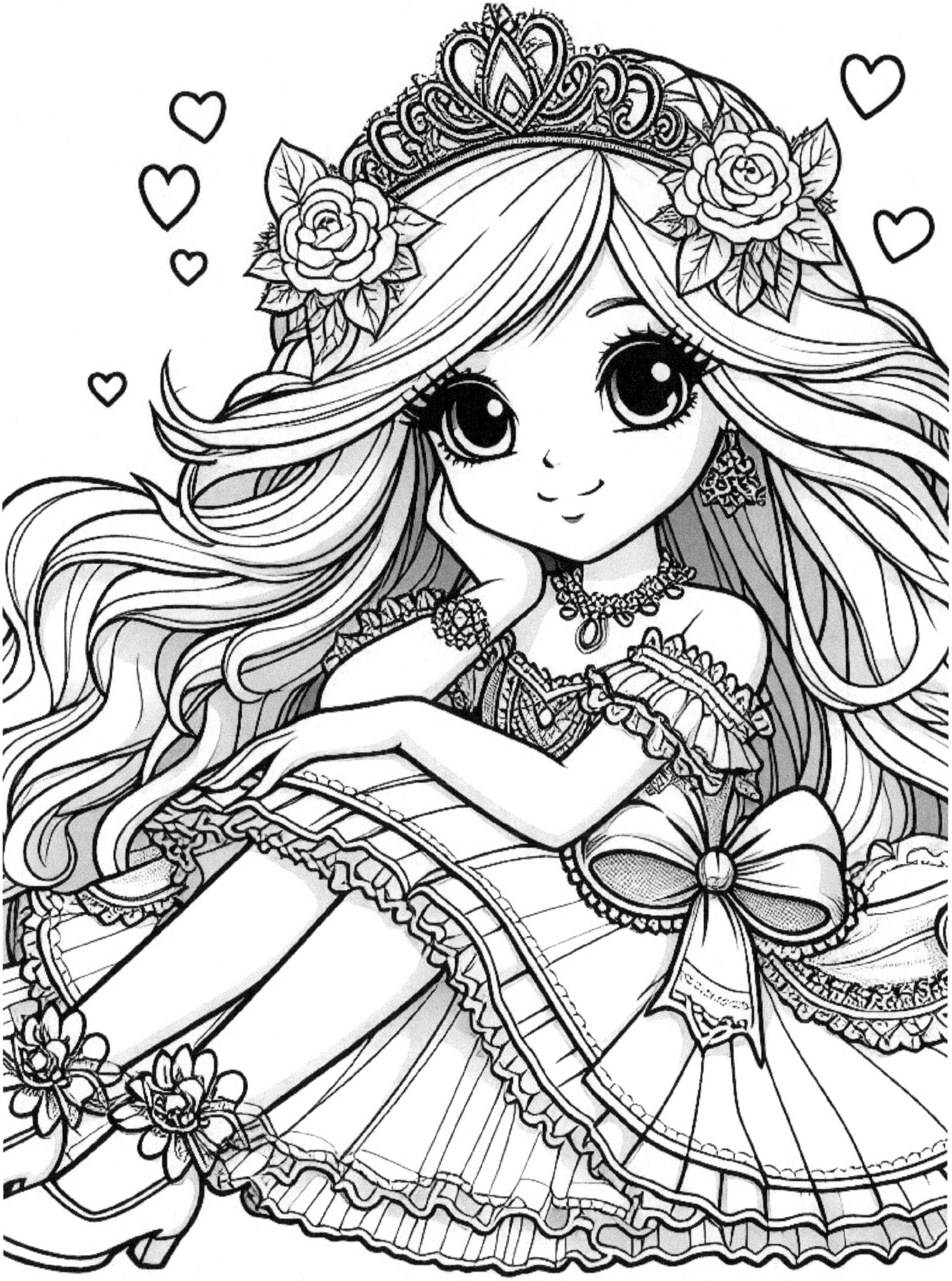

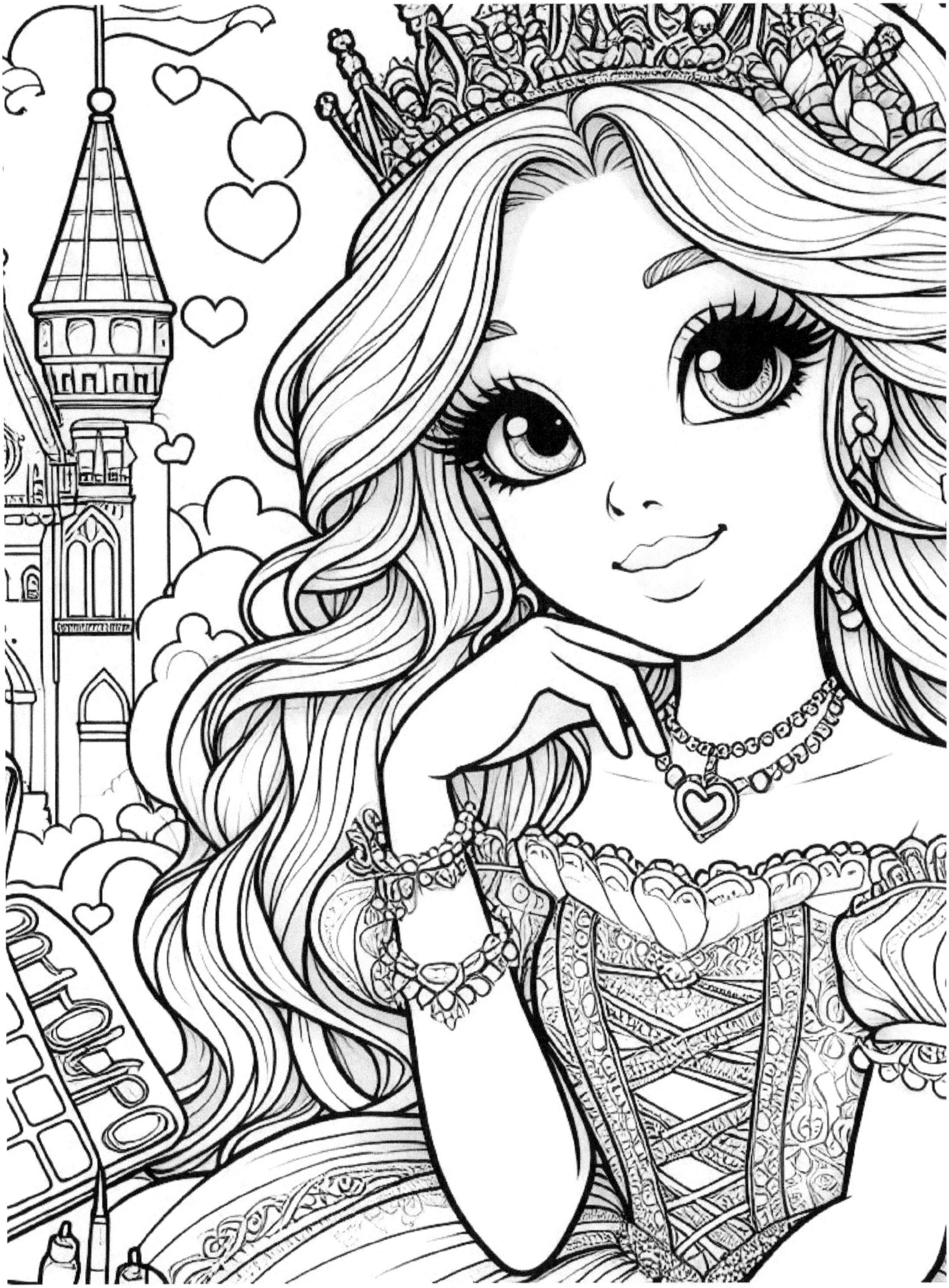

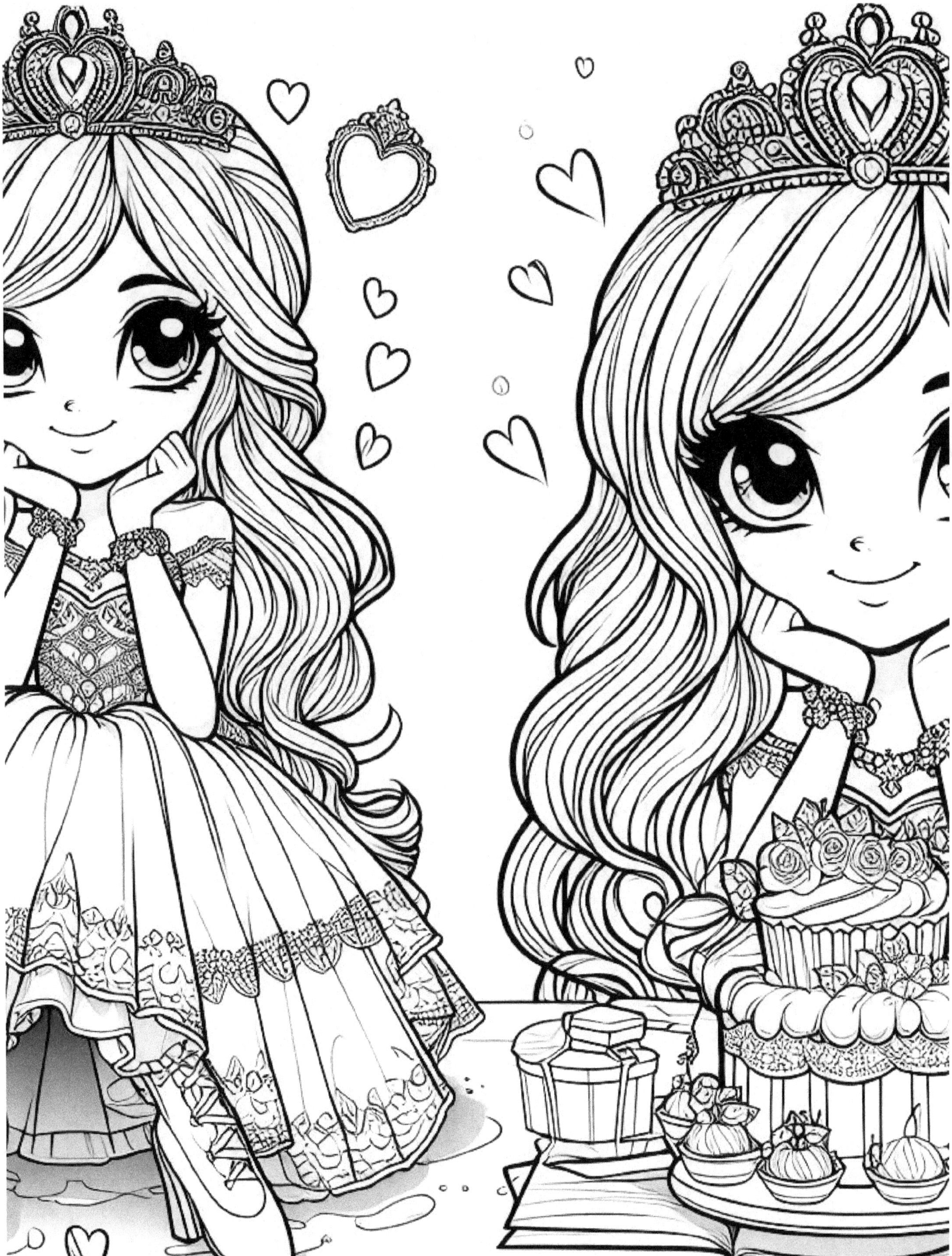

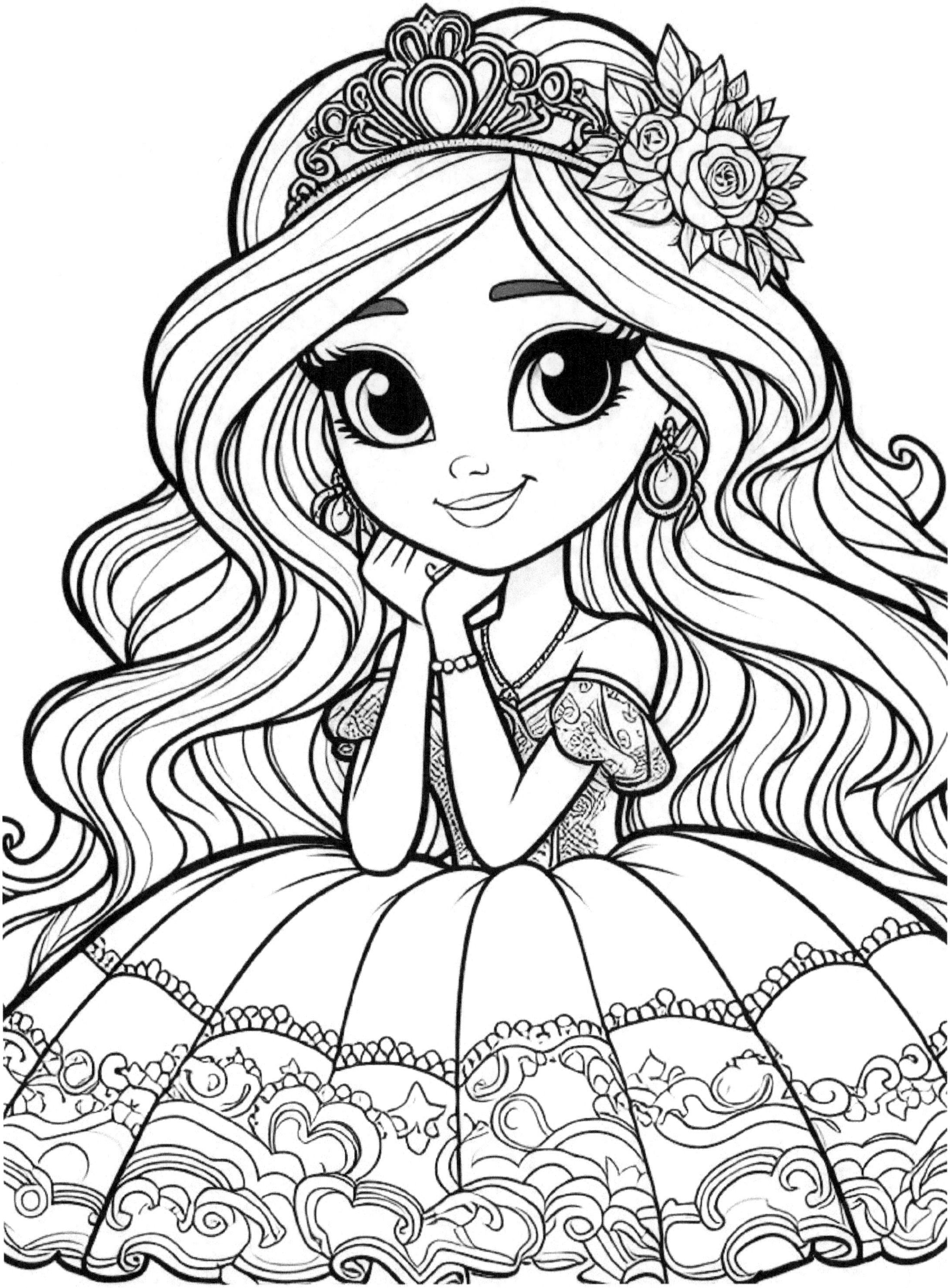

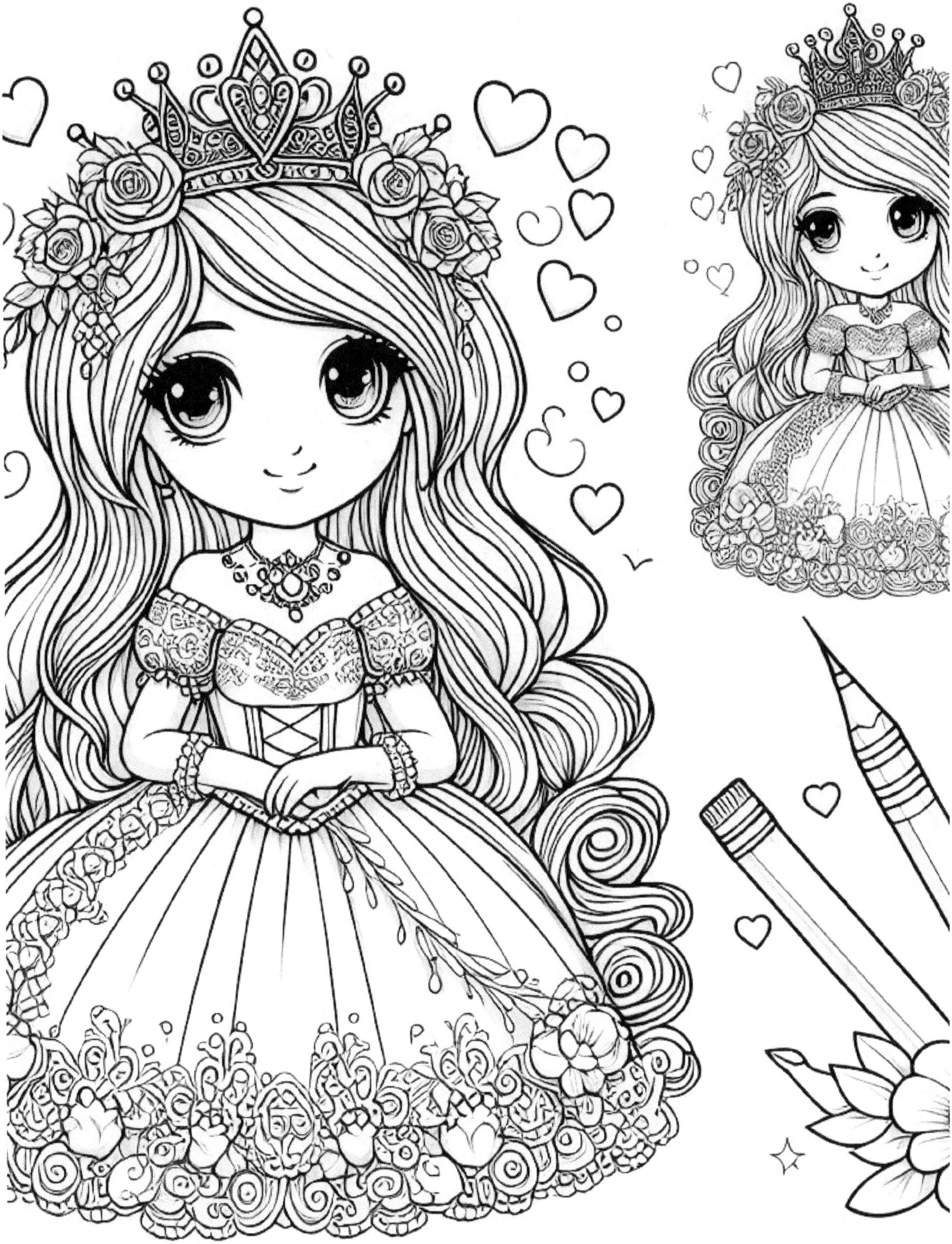

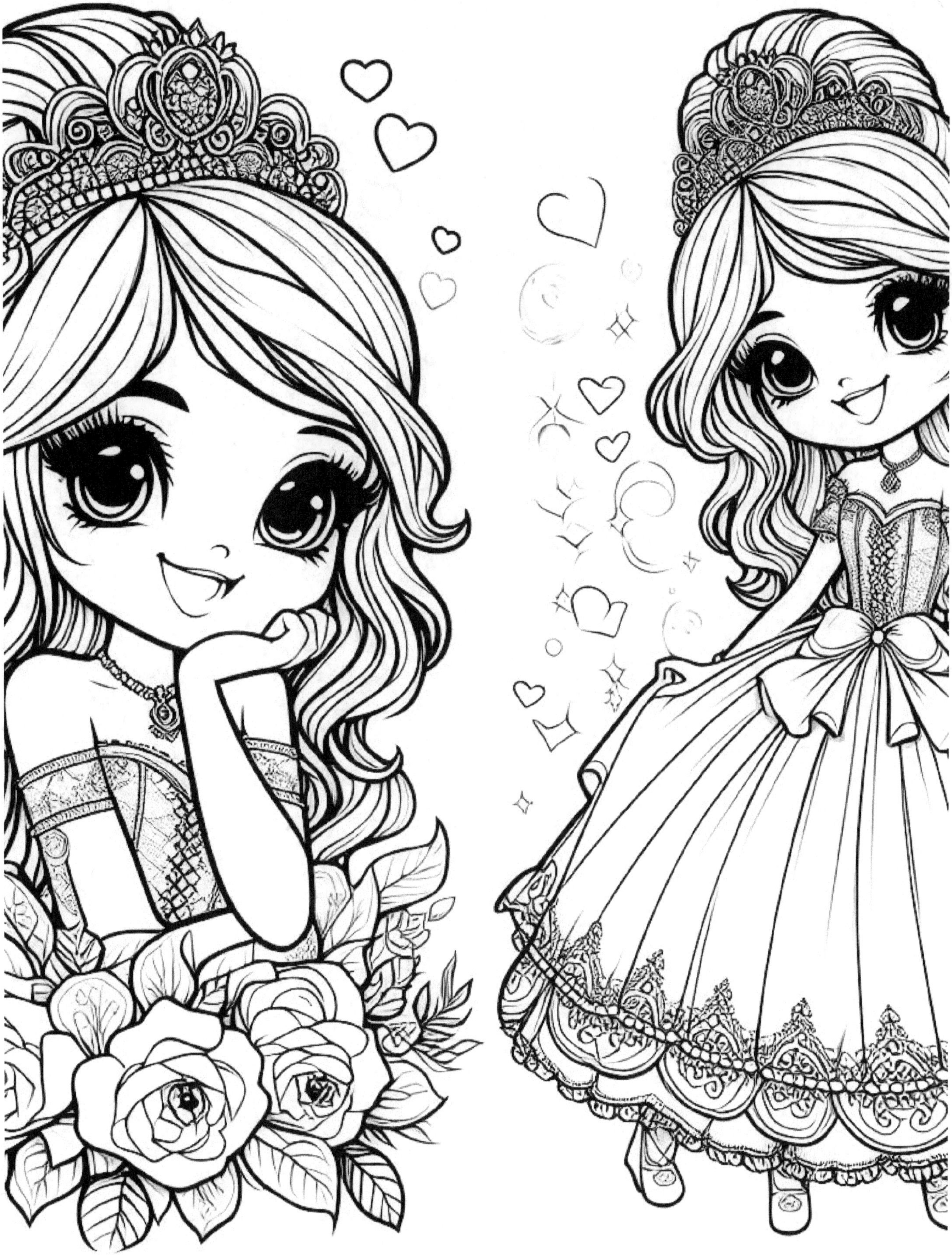

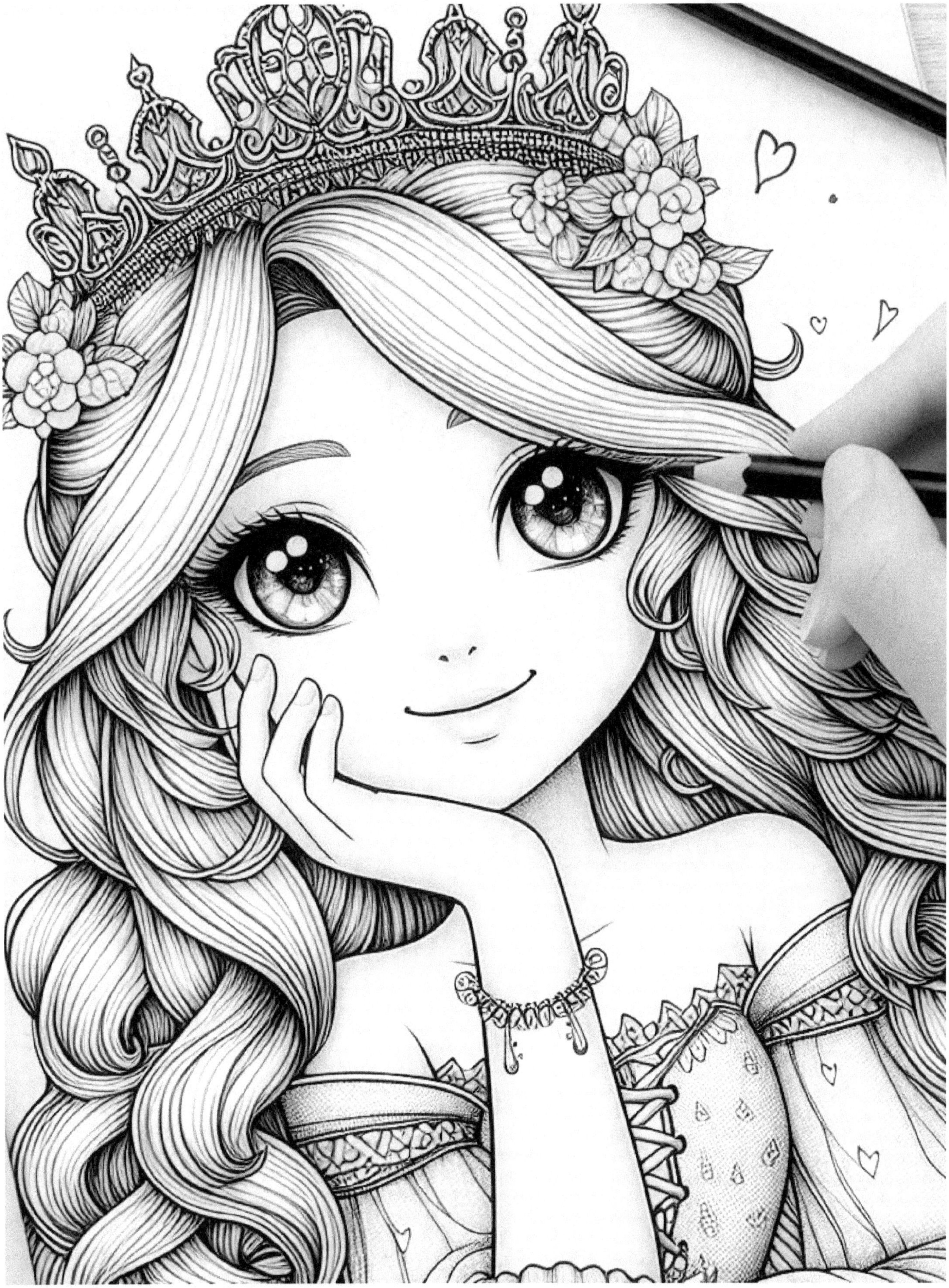

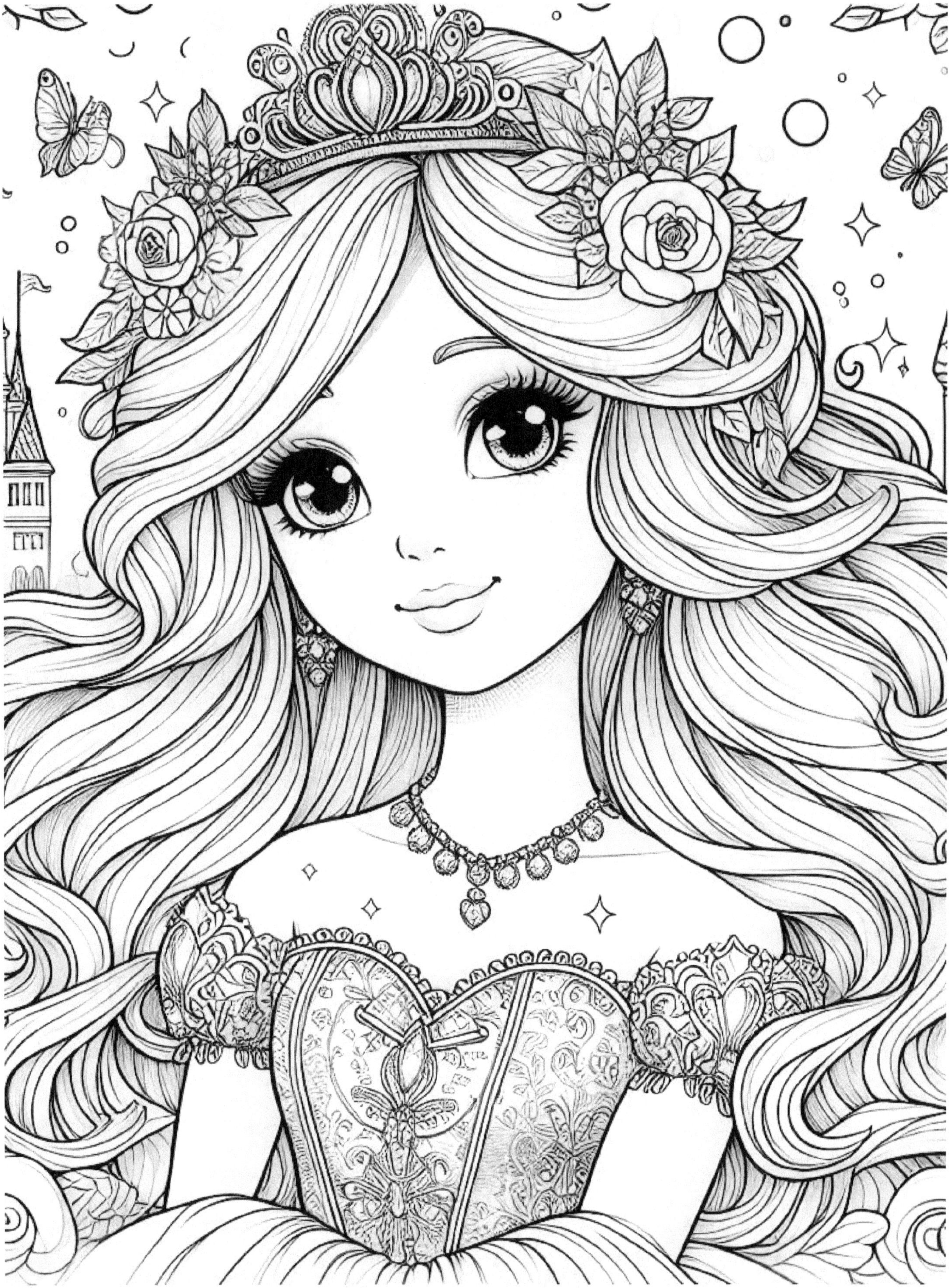

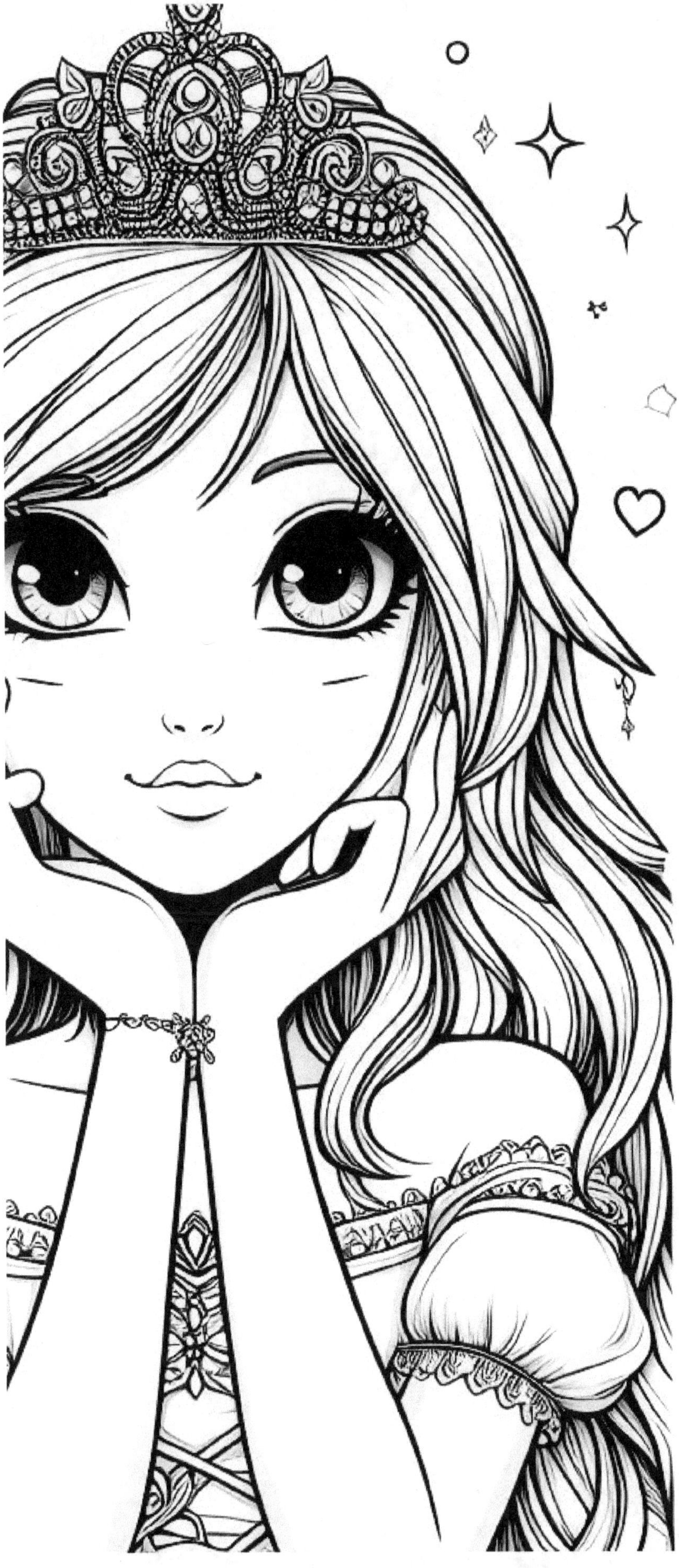
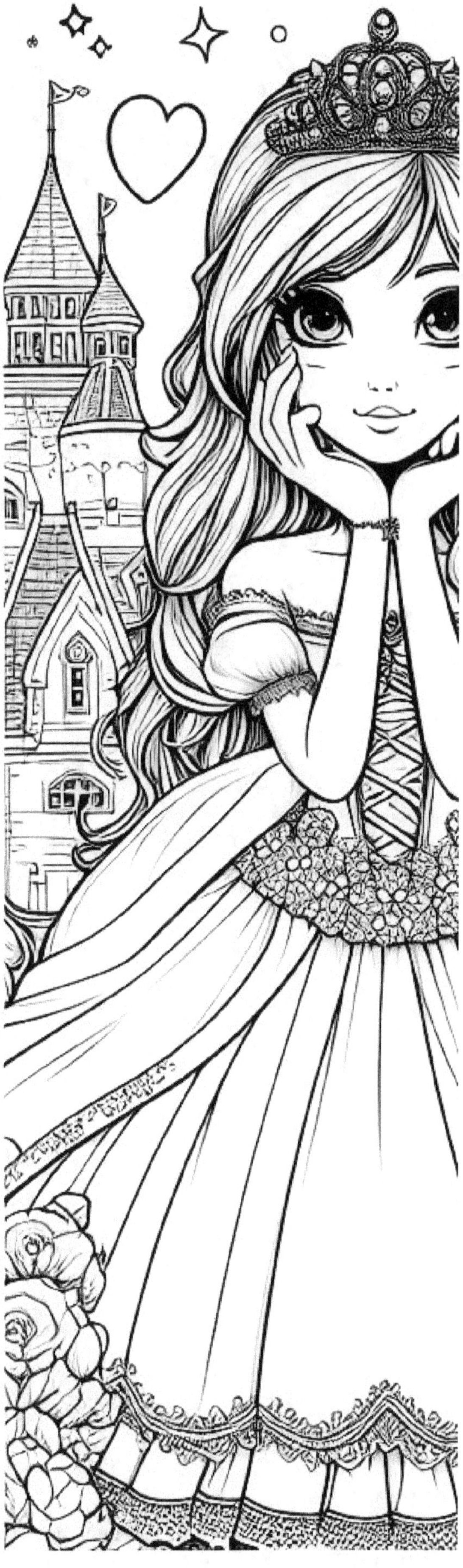

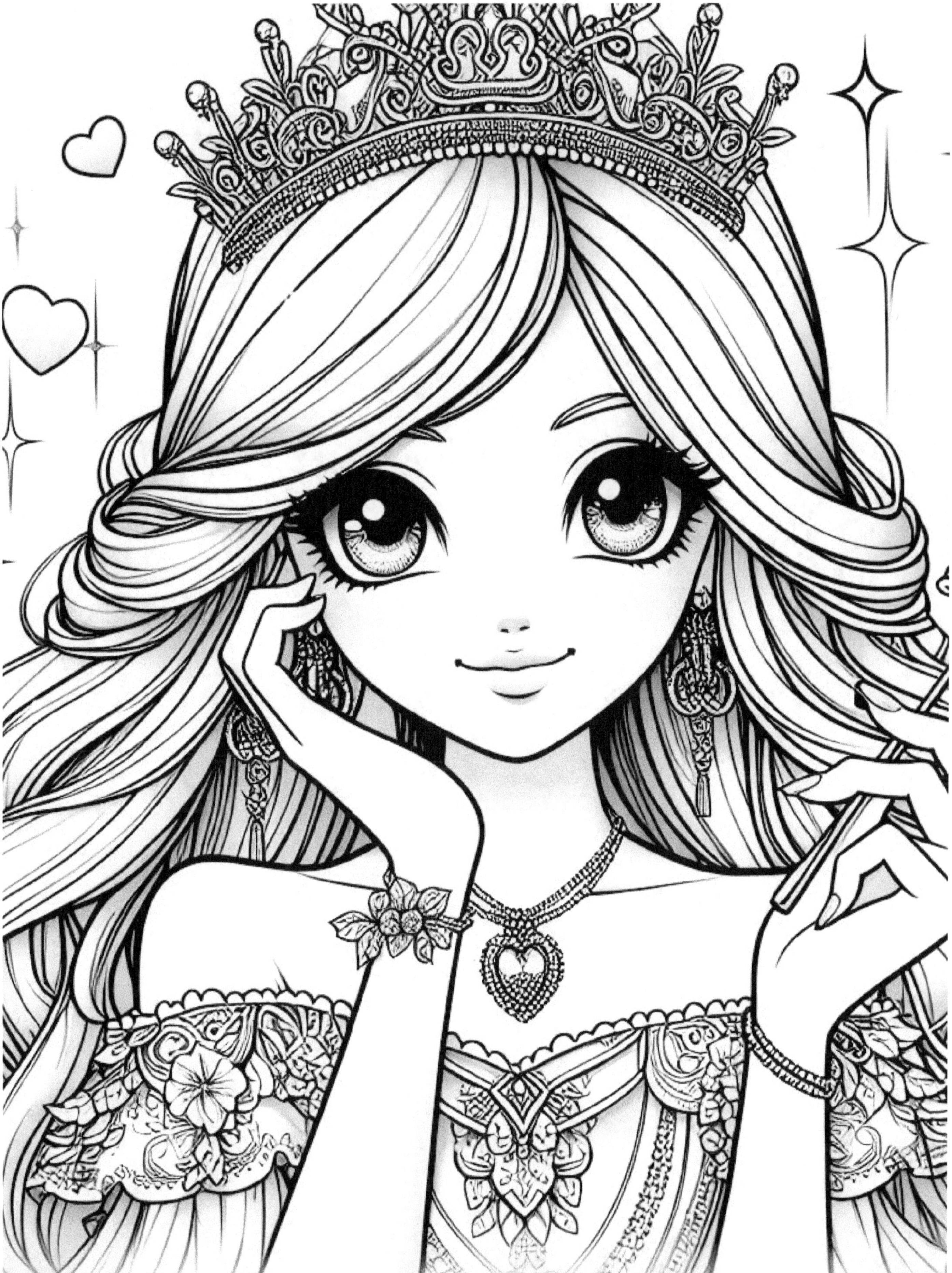

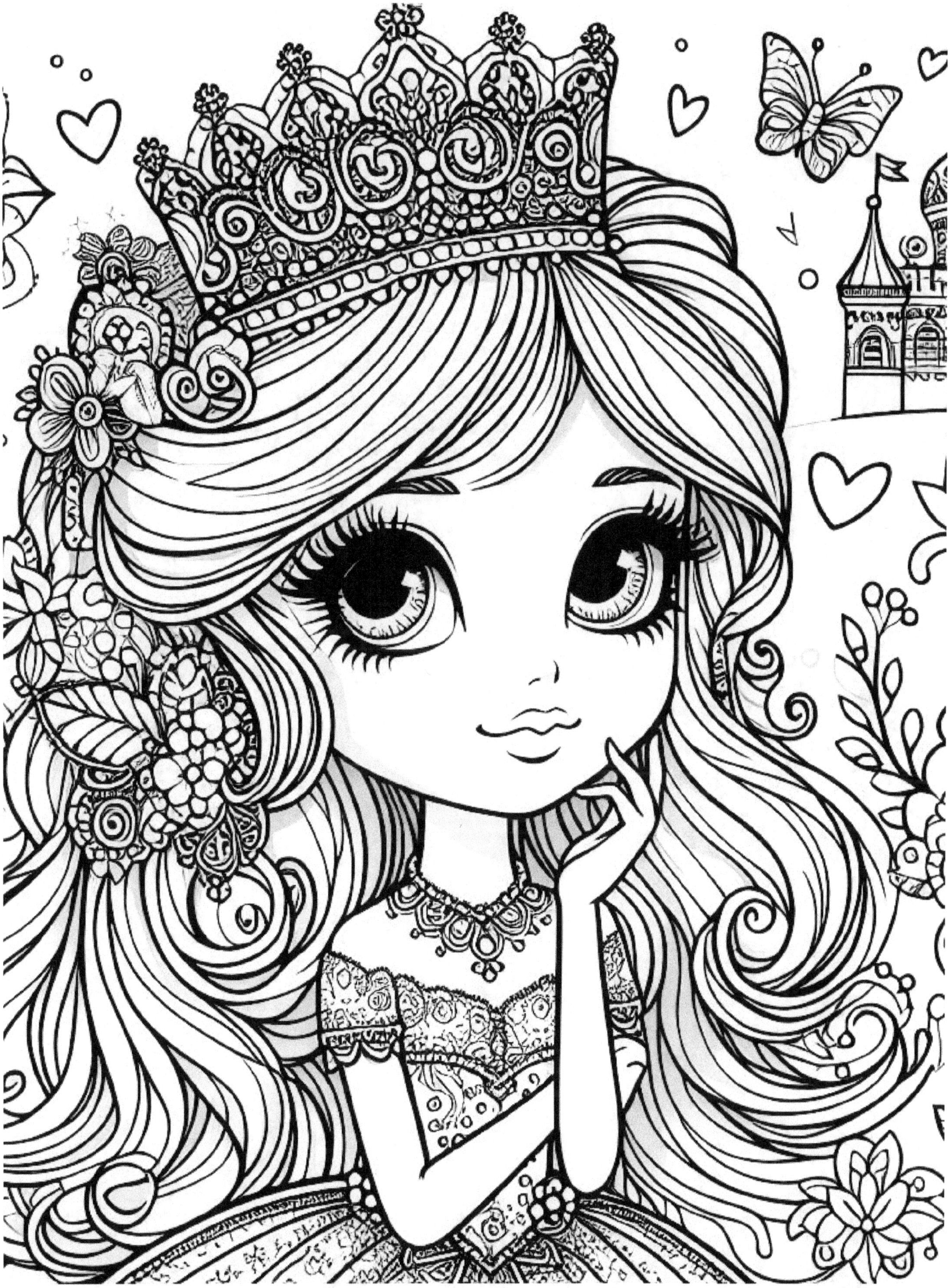

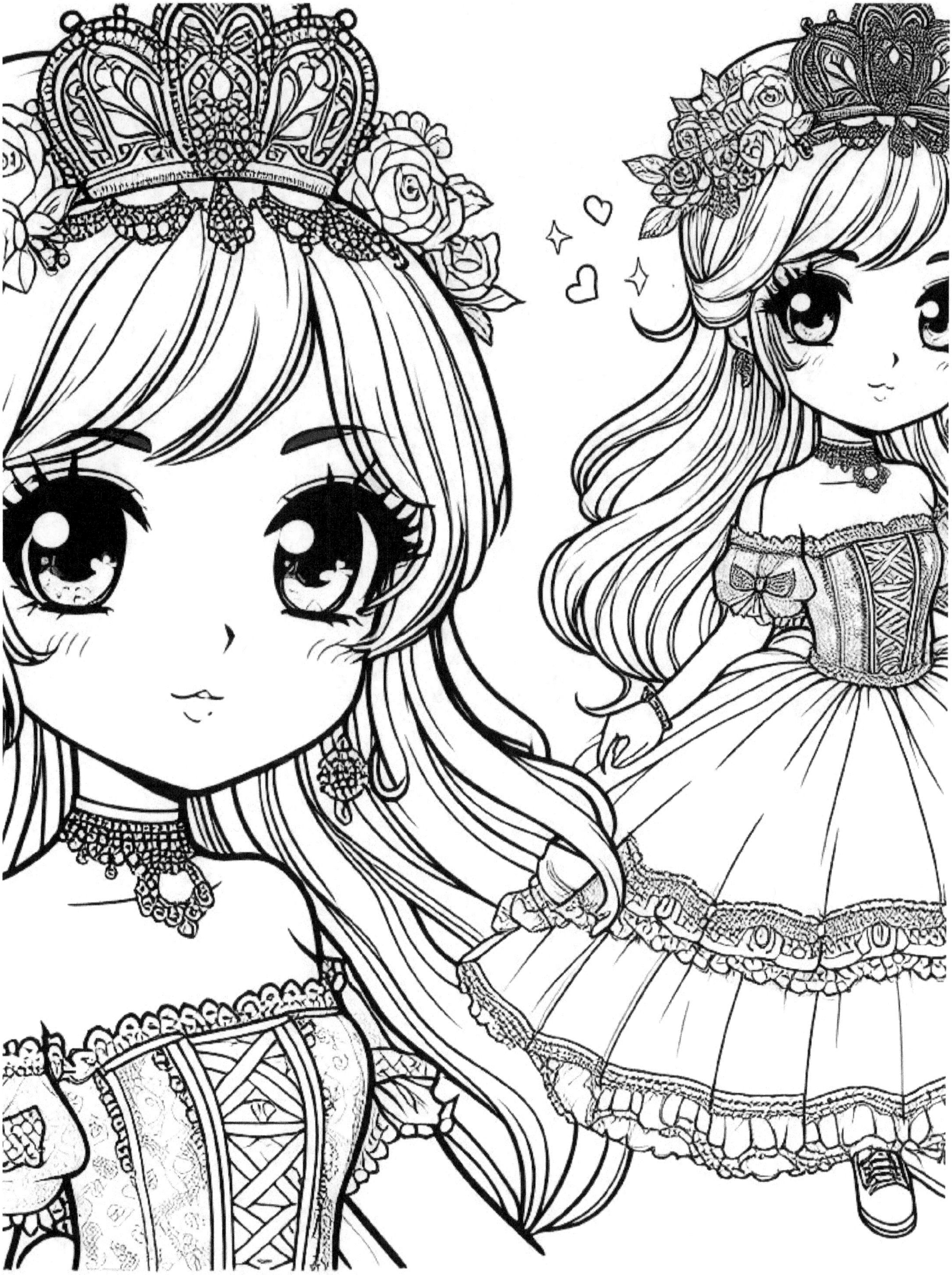

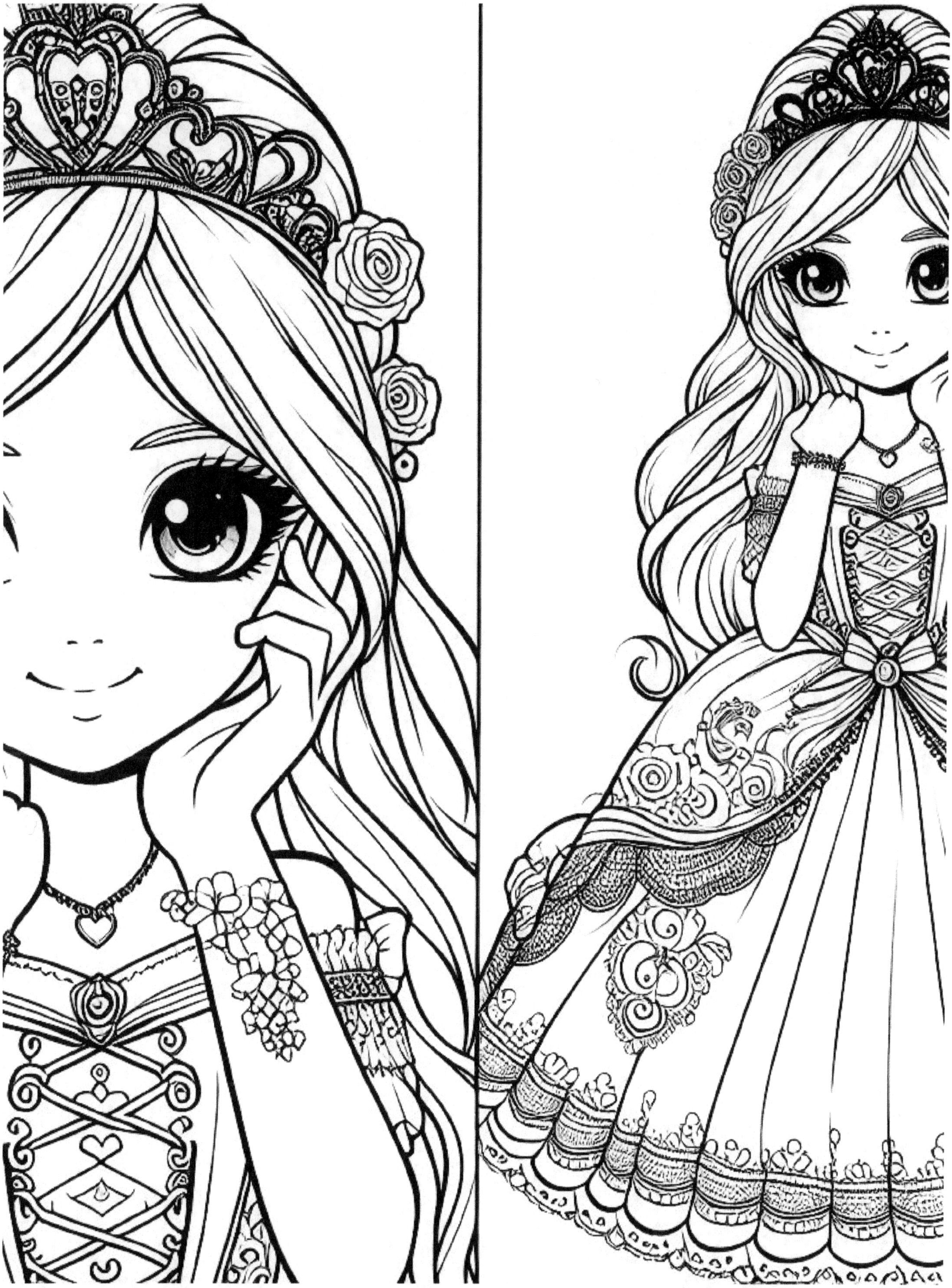

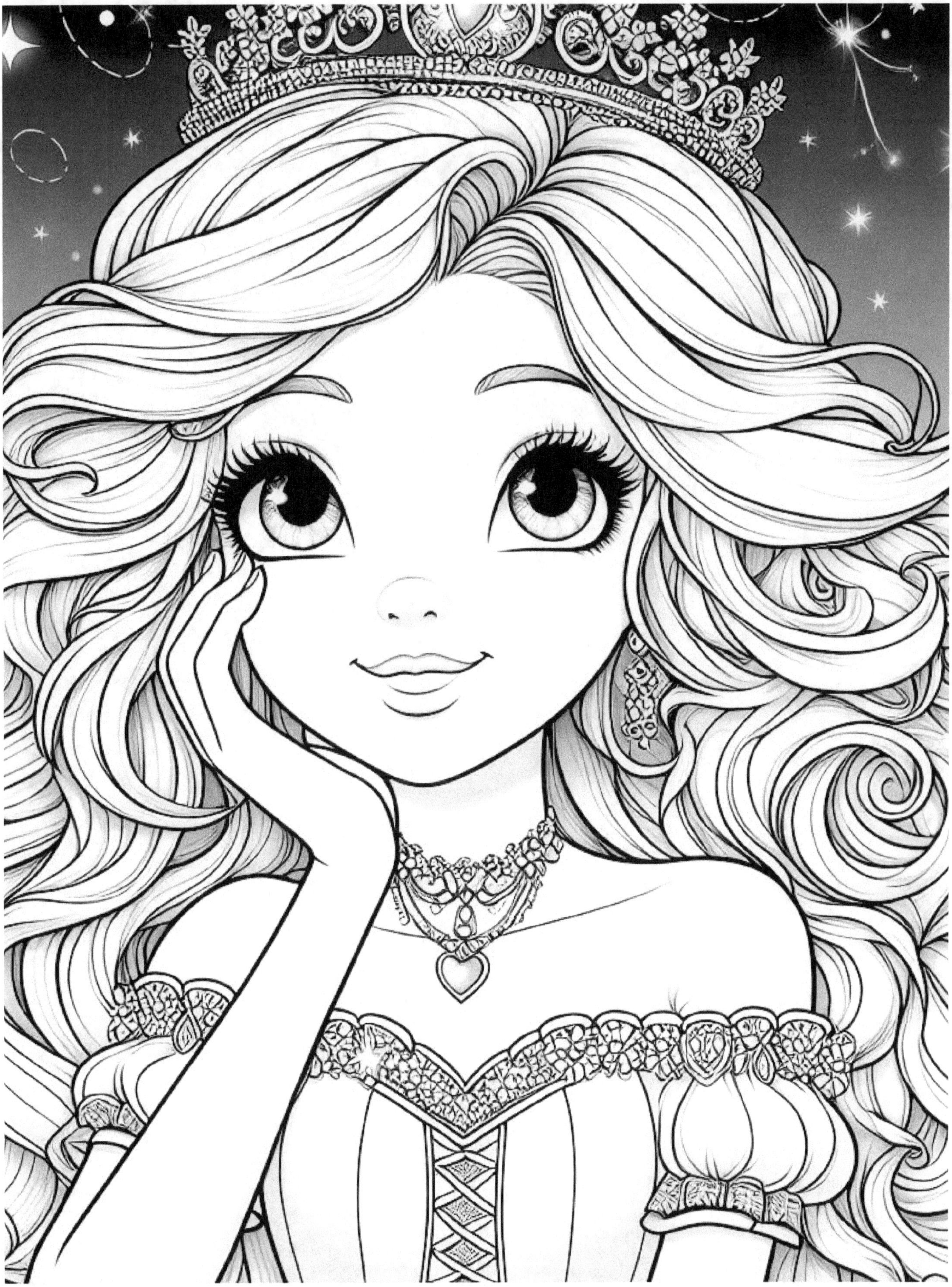

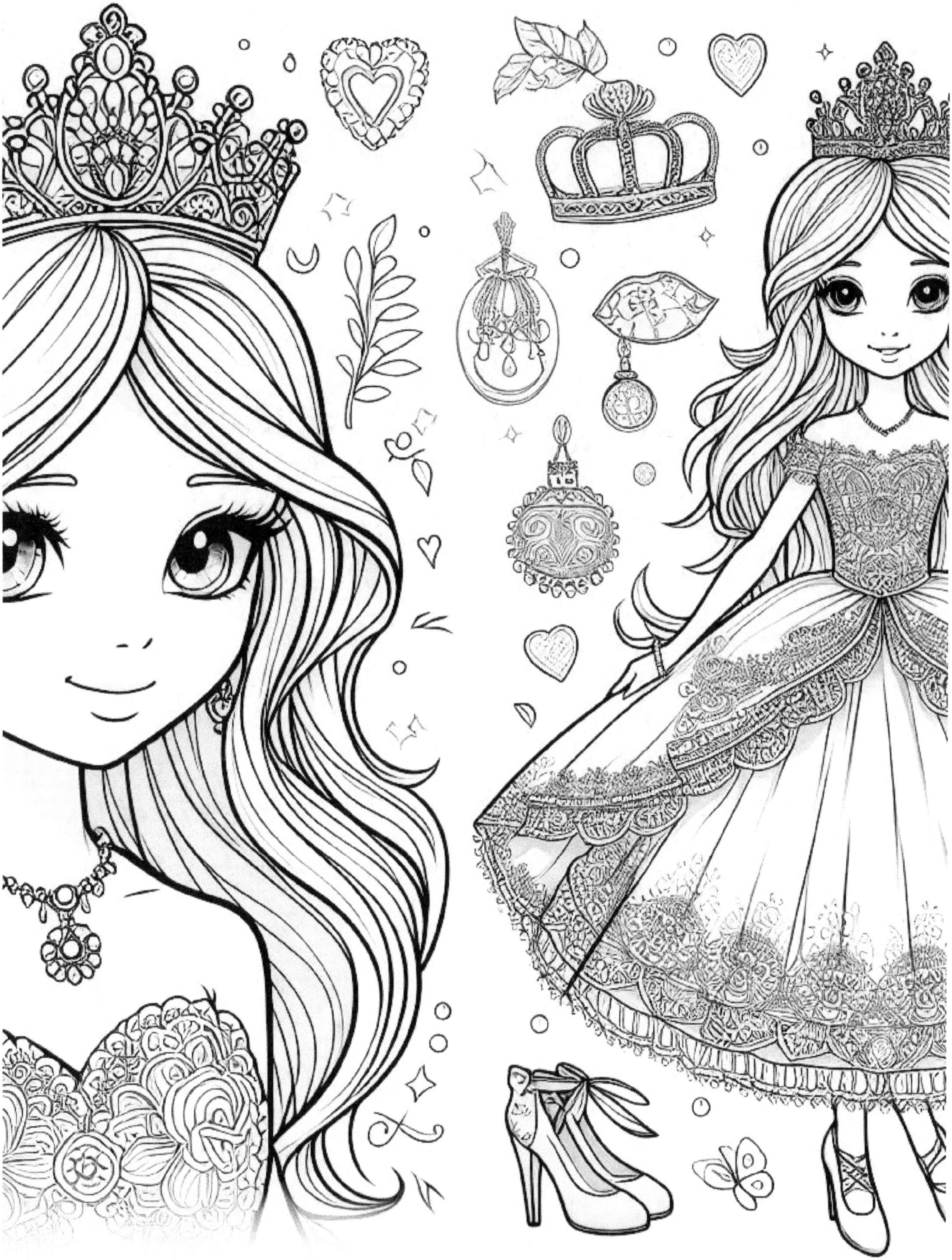

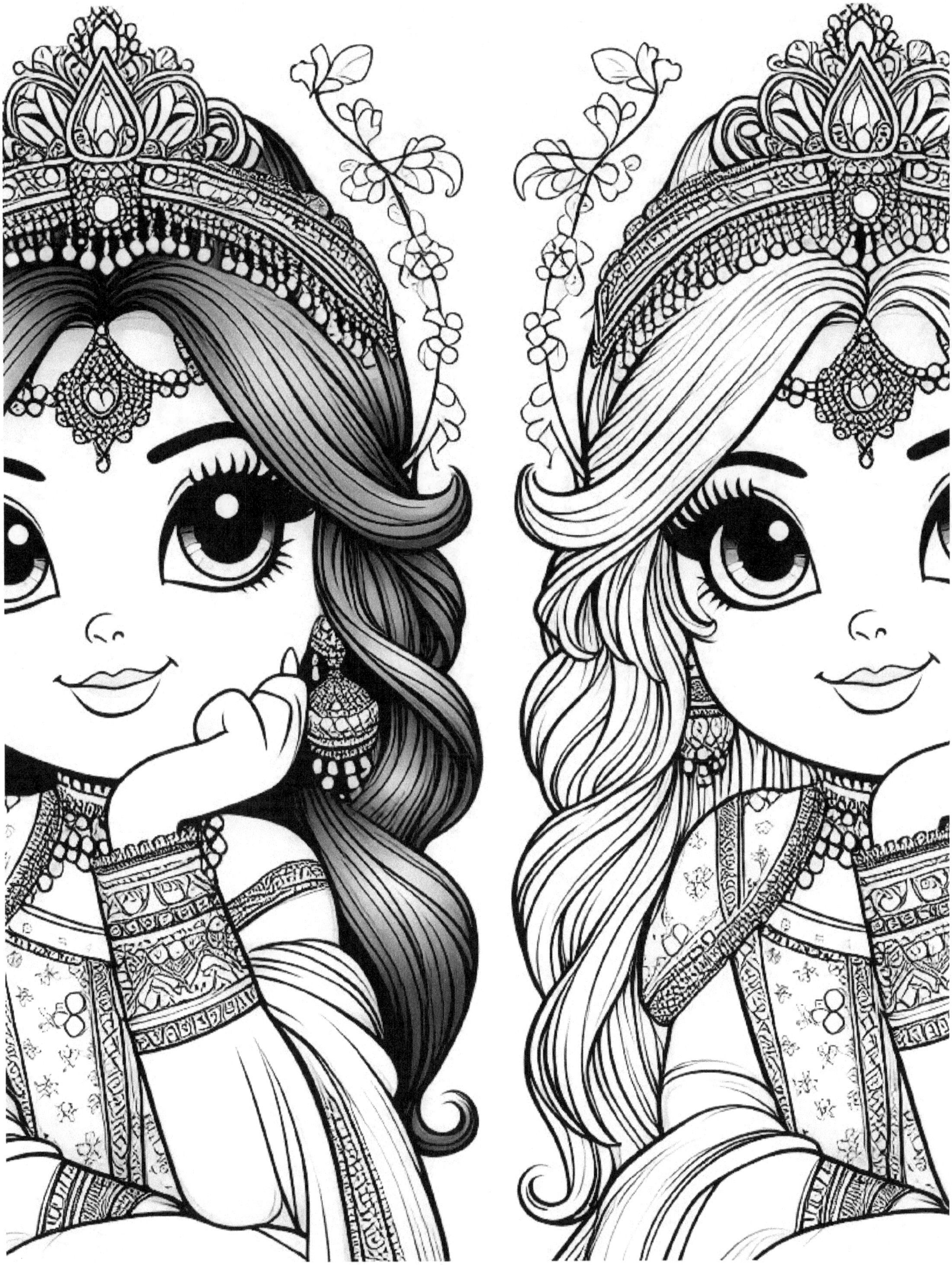

www.ingramcontent.com/pod-product-compliance
Lightning Source LLC
Chambersburg PA
CBHW062125220526
45471CB00010B/3877
* 9 7 9 8 3 2 3 9 3 7 3 4 9 *